How to Beat the Claw Machine

By Brian McKanna

Legal & Disclaimer

The content and information in this book is consistent and truthful, and it has been provided for informational, educational and business purposes only.

The content and information contained in this book has been compiled from reliable sources, which are accurate based on the knowledge, belief, expertise, and information of the Author. The author cannot be held liable for any omissions and/or errors.

Table of Contents

How to Beat the Claw Machine: Tips and Tricks to help you Win Big!

3

Dedication

This book is dedicated to my parents for always giving me a few dollars to play the claw machine.

And to the love of my life, who I met behind the prize counter on my first day of work at Six Flags.

About the Author

I've been addicted to claw machines since my first win at the age of 5. Growing up I spent countless hours in the arcade, developing the knowledge and skill it takes to consistently beat the infamous crane. At age 17, I started my own arcade company and grew it to 4 locations and over 20 machines. Hands on experience taught me how to repair crane machines and other arcade games. I was later recruited by the world's largest claw machine manufacture to maintain and fix all the arcade and claw machines inside Six Flags St. Louis.

INTRODUCTION

First off, I'd like to take a minute and say **CONGRAGULATIONS**! You just invested in your future in the best way possible. Winning the claw machine does so much more than you think. For example, it helps boost your self-esteem; there is something powerful and fulfilling in being a winner. Seeing your prize drop into the open, clear box is a once-in-a-lifetime experience, unless you know the secrets! Thankfully for you, I've spent my entire life playing and learning everything there is to know about the almighty claw. Prepare to impress your family, friends, and maybe even that special someone...

My wife Kat and I standing inside The Big One Claw (2015)

Let's kick things off by going over what you'll be learning:

Lesson 1: We will discuss crane machines, the different types, how they work, and how they are programmed against you.

Lesson 2: The arcade's you'll encounter, lingo you need to know, and the three basic observations you should make before inserting your money.

Lesson 3: How to pick your target, the biggest tip you need to know to be successful while playing the claw, and the follow-through strategy.

Lesson 4: Some situations you may run into and secret techniques to outwit any claw.

Lesson 5: We will wrap it up with how to put your new knowledge into practice.

 Claw school is in session!

How to Beat the Claw Machine: Tips and Tricks to help you Win Big!

LESSON 1

CLAW MACHINE 101

How to Beat the Claw Machine: Tips and Tricks to help you Win Big!

What are claw machines?

Claw machines are some of the most unique games on the planet. Think of them as miniature stores filled with all kinds of cool prizes just waiting to be won. And just like people, crane machines come in many different shapes, sizes, and varieties. The most common machine is the classic stuffed plush version with a claw and prize shoot. I call this the OC (original claw). But there are many other types of claws, including jewelry, winner-every-time, candy, high-end electronic, up-over, UFO, the list goes on and on! There are hundreds of different crane machines throughout the world. In this book, we will focus on the most common and my personal favorite, the OC.

How they work

It will come as no surprise that, like everything else in our modern world, claw machines are controlled by an internal computer. They use specialized software coded specifically for crane machines. Every claw manufacture is different, but they all have in common the ability to give false hope. They are programmed to be difficult while leaving you just enough hope that you might win a prize with just a few more dollars.

To answer the question almost everyone asks me, **YES**, most claw machines are rigged. The good news is **we can outsmart them!** As an arcade technician, I was instructed to program all the claw machines with a 3 second hold. A 3 second hold is where the crane picks up the prize and after three seconds in the air drops it back onto the playing field,

9

How to Beat the Claw Machine: Tips and Tricks to help you Win Big!

crushing your sole. A claw machine will only have enough strength to win once the machine has made enough money. The internal computer keeps track of all the money put in the machine and only allows someone to win once it hits a predetermined amount of money. Once enough money has been put in, the claw will be given full strength allowing someone to win a prize. Does that mean you have no hope of winning if the machine isn't ready to pay off? **NO FREAKIN' WAY!** I'm going to teach you how to beat the odds and conquer the claw.

10

How to Beat the Claw Machine: Tips and Tricks to help you Win Big!

How are claw machines programmed against you?

Claw machines are programed with common mathematical calculations designed to ensure profits for the machine's owner. As much as I love arcade games, the goal in owning claw machines for me was always to make money (and fund my claw machine addiction). The more money I made, the more machine's I could buy!

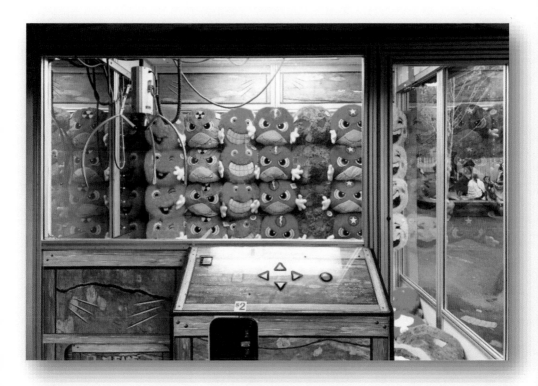

The Calculation

1) 100 plays × $0.50 per play = $50

2) $50 × 10% payout = $45 must be inserted before someone can win

3) The game will only pay out once it has reached a 90% profit

LESSON 2

ARCADE 101

How to Beat the Claw Machine: Tips and Tricks to help you Win Big!

It may feel like arcades have been around forever, but it wasn't until 1971 that the first arcade game was invented. It was called Computer Space and looked like this

Created by Nolan Bushnell and Ted Dabney in 1971, it was the first arcade video game as well as the first commercially available video game. It featured a rocket controlled by the player, engaged in a missile battle with a pair of hardware-controlled flying saucers set against a starfield background. The game is enclosed in a custom fiberglass cabinet, which Bushnell designed to look futuristic.

Little did its inventors know that this game would start a revolution in entertainment, one that is still growing and thriving over 50 years later! Arcades, like claw machines, come in many different varieties. There is everything from the giant Dave & Busters to the local mom and pop hole in the wall to just a few machines sitting at the entrance of Wal-Mart.

There are some arcades focused solely on winning tickets which are exchanged for prizes. For example, Chuck E. Cheese does not offer any redemption games (machines you can win prizes directly out of) instead players earn tickets based on how well they play. Other arcades offer only redemption games. Most popular of all are blended arcades, where both ticket and redemption games live in harmony.

Lingo you need to know

Enough arcade talk…let's get back to **the claw!**

While playing the crane machine make sure not to stab and always take advantage of any opportunity to rake. If you understood that last sentence you are well versed in claw lingo and more than likely have trash bags full of stuffed animals in your basement. Most likely though, that sentence made no sense. Therefore, here are a few terms you should know before embarking on your claw journey so that you are able to identify some of the things that will happen during play.

Plush - A broad term for any kind of stuffed animal.

This is a word I picked up while working for Six Flags. Instead of saying stuffed animals, my boss and co-workers would say plush. Plush is a more universal term that can be used to describe any kind of stuffed animal.

How to Beat the Claw Machine: Tips and Tricks to help you Win Big!

Shoot - The compartment inside a crane machine that plush is dropped into when a prize is won.

The shoot is located directly under the resting position of the claw. In most cases, the shoot and the claw are on the front left side of the machine. The shoot is your friend and your enemy. Sometimes it will help you out by propping up plush in a good position. Other times you'll stab it and waste your turn.

Stabbing – When one or more of the prongs lands on the prize causing the crane to prematurely close.

This is going to happen...a lot. It's just part of the game. To win, you will have to take some risks, drop the claw at weird angles, and inevitably stab the very prize you love so dearly. Stabbing almost always results in a loss. The crane is programmed to squeeze and lift once it hits a solid

How to Beat the Claw Machine: Tips and Tricks to help you Win Big!

surface. Because you have hit the top of your target, or another plush getting in your way, the crane will not continue dropping and has almost no chance of getting low enough to grab your stuffed animal. Your best bet is to learn which way the claw spins. They can twirl both left and right, so on your first attempt, take note of which direction it moves and where the prongs of the claw end up. This will help you line up the claw more accurately and ovoid the frustration of a stab.

Raking – Using the claw to push plush across the playing field without dropping the claw.

This is by far one of my favorite situations to encounter! The only way you can rake is if the plush is stacked high enough for the claw to reach them without being deployed. You'll usually find this situation right after they have restocked the crane machine. Your goal while raking is to push the plush either directly into the shoot for an instant win or onto its side for a better shot. We will dive deeper into this technique in lesson 4.

Swinging – Using the joystick to swing the claw back and forth to win prizes outside the playing field.

This technique is used when you need to reach an area of the playing field that isn't obtainable within the normal parameters of the claw. Often, I will use this technique when going for something pushed up against the glass or when there is a large plush in front of the one I am aiming for.

16

How to Beat the Claw Machine: Tips and Tricks to help you Win Big!

Not every crane will allow you to swing, but the ones that do are extra fun! More info to come on this in lesson 4.

The three BIG questions

Before you put your money into a crane machine, there are three things you should ask yourself. These questions will help you determine whether you are going to waste your money or not.

How is the plush stacked?

This makes a HUGE difference in your ability to win. The most optimal way to beat the claw is to pick up stuffed animals from a horizontal position. When the plush is on its side, you have the most space and leverage for the claw to get fully underneath your prize. This is an important part of my' beat the claw' strategy, explained in lesson 3.

How picked over is the plush?

You can usually tell when a machine has just been stocked vs after it has seen some winners. When a machine has been picked over it can be a good indication that the claw has enough strength to win. On the other hand, a fully stocked machine provides more options to choose from. You can still win on a freshly stocked machine even though it may pose more challenging.

How much per play?

Over the years crane machine prices have risen at a steady pace. The most common price per play back in the mid-2000's was $0.50; today most machines charge $1 per play. At that price, it may be wise to take a quick scan of the machine to determine if what's inside is worth the price you'll be paying.

LESSON 3

Claw Skill Training

How to Beat the Claw Machine: Tips and Tricks to help you Win Big!

This is where the real fun begins!

In this lesson I will reveal the strategy that has consistently helped me beat the claw for the last two decades. But first...

Picking your target

You have found a claw machine you'd like to play. You know how much it cost, and you have your eye on a few awesome stuffed animals inside you are dying to take home. This is your moment! Here is what you need to consider when picking your prize:

Think about the shape of the plush you are targeting. **IS IT ROUND? Does it have arms or legs?** Does it have a big nose? Is there anything you can hook on-to? These are all big considerations because you must use every feature of the stuffed animal to your advantage. Work smarter, not harder!

The best style of plush to go after is something with a small waist and a big head. Your best bet is to go for the waist, which will (hopefully) allow the claw to get fully under the body and close completely. In the best-case scenario, the claw remains closed while lifting and moving over the shoot, and you win the prize. The head is a great secondary option. If you're able to get the prongs of the claw under a nose or ear, your odds of winning go up. Make sure to keep your eye out for something to hook onto, whether it's an arm, or leg or the sleeve of the prize's shirt. Be creative when it comes to your approach and pick your prize wisely.

The #1 trick you need to know

Two-angle approach

Almost every claw machine has a mirror on its back wall. This feature serves two purposes. First, it makes the machine look bigger than it is. Second and most importantly, the mirror messes with your depth perception. When you see the reflection of the claw in the mirror it may appear to be directly on top of the prize you're going for when in fact, it isn't.

What you need to focus on is the claw itself. Never use the mirror to line up your shot! Instead, look from the sides of the crane machine to position the claw directly over your target. I call this the two-angle approach. You'll want to first aim the claw over the prize from the front of the machine. Once you believe you're precisely over the plush, quickly walk or lean your head around to one of the sides of the machine. Make sure that you are truly over your target. By doing this, you are lining up your shot from both angles, guaranteeing that you will land directly on your target. This trick alone will increase your odds of winning tenfold! If you have someone with you, have them stand at the side of the machine and instruct you on where to move the claw. My dad, brother and I have used this method for years with a ton of success!

Incorporate this technique into every one of your attempts at the claw. Even if you think your aim is dead-on, it never hurts to give it a second look. Throughout my 20 plus years playing the claw machine, I have yet to find a better and more reliable strategy than this. Despite the two-angle approach, there is still the possibility you won't win on your first try, which leads us into our next section on the follow-through strategy.

The follow-through strategy

The follow-through strategy consists of sticking with a prize until you have it in your hands. Let's run through a common scenario. On your first try, you aim the claw, drop it onto your target and pick it up only for it to be dropped a second later. At this point, some people bail and assume that the prize isn't winnable. I'm here to say stick with it! If the claw picked up your prize once, it could do it again. In most situations, picking up and dropping a stuffed animal will get it in a better position to be won. They usually roll onto their sides or back after being dropped, which, as we know is a great position for the plush to be in. Playing claw machines can be tricky and often requires several attempts along with lots of strategy. Using the two-angle approach and the follow-through technique will help increase your odds of winning the fun and challenging game of claw machines.

My brother Tommy and I at our neighborhood arcade, The Infield, back in the early 2000's

How to Beat the Claw Machine: Tips and Tricks to help you Win Big!

LESSON 4

Claw Skill Training

How to Beat the Claw Machine: Tips and Tricks to help you Win Big!

Situations you'll encounter

Packed in tight: <u>When there is too much plush in the machine</u>

This is the absolute worst situation you can encounter. When there are too many prizes stuffed into the claw machine it becomes virtually impossible to win anything. As we've discussed in previous lessons, the claw needs to have room under the plush to pick it up. When they are packed in too tight, there is no room for the claw to make its way under your prize. An indicator that a machine is packed too tight is when all the plush is standing directly up and none (from what you can tell) have been won. It's always better if a few stuffed animals have already been won because you'll have more room to pick up your desired prize.

Empty machine: <u>When all or almost all the prizes have been won out of a claw.</u>

This is a situation you won't encounter much. I've seen it a few dozen times over the years, and it's a little shocking. One of two things has happened in this situation. One, the claw's strength is set way too high, it's super easy to win. Two, whoever is responsible for stocking the claw hasn't added plush in a long time. If you encounter an empty machine in an established arcade like a Dave n' Busters, find someone who works there and ask if they can refill the machine. If you believe the claw is just

25

How to Beat the Claw Machine: Tips and Tricks to help you Win Big!

super easy to win, keep that in mind next time you see that machine stocked up and empty it!

Big $ prizes: <u>Prizes inside the claw worth more than $100.</u>

This has become HUGE in the last few years. Many crane machines, specifically inside amusement parks and large chain arcades, offer expensive prizes. These prizes go from gaming consoles to iPhones to $100 gift cards and even designer purses. I recently played a crane machine filled with Michael Kors purses that retailed for around $500 each. Often these machines won't have the actual prizes in them, rather small blocks with a picture of the prize on them that you use to redeem your actual prize at the ticket counter. I maintained several of these machines at Six Flags, and here is what I know about them: they are very hard to win and will only pay out once they are ready. We only gave away a handful of large prizes every year at Six Flags.

Claw machines are *always* breaking down!

This claw pictured was chronically broke in my career with Six Flags. I could never figure out what was wrong with it. With lots of moving parts, claw machines tend to break often. Thank you arcade technicians!

In lesson 1, we talked about how crane machines must make a certain predetermined amount of money before they give the claw enough strength to pick up the prize. That principle is the same with these big $ prize claws, but the margins are much larger. Instead of needing $20 to pay out a prize, they often need around $2,000 before the machine is ready to let someone win. Trust me, these machines are still worth playing! Even though your odds of winning these claws are extremely low, there is still a slim chance you might win. You have no idea how many people have played this game before you or when it last paid off. My thought is, if I put $2 or $3 in and lose, no big deal. But if I put $2 or $3 in and win, I just got myself an amazing prize for only a few bucks! It's a gamble, but a gamble worth taking in my opinion.

Plush > claw: <u>When the plush inside a machine is larger than the claw can open.</u>

As crazy as it sounds, some claw owners/operators have plush inside their machines that are WAY too big for the size of the claw. This isn't something you'll see every day, although it is still very prevalent. I'd like to think claw machine owners just aren't paying attention, but my suspicion is they do this so that no one has a chance of winning. If a stuffed animal is 2 feet wide and the claw is only 1 foot wide, you have a very low chance of winning. Your only chance of getting anything is by hooking onto the plush somehow.

SECRET TECHNIQUES

The Swing technique

Although it is advised in chapter three to avoid prizes leaning up against the glass, they're still achievable through the swing technique. The swing technique doesn't work on every claw, but it will on some. The premise is to quickly move the claw back and forth, allowing it to swing. While the claw is still moving, hit the drop button timing it so that the claw lands where you need it to. It'll take you a few tries to figure out when to drop the claw so that the timing of the swing matches perfectly with the area you are aiming for. This is great when going for a prize out of normal claw reach, when you're aiming for the side of a prize or when you're trying to knock something over.

Raking technique

This is a personal favorite of mine. The crane machine has just been filled and all the plush is standing straight up at attention, ready to be won. The prizes at the very back of the machine are usually tall enough to be pushed over with the claw without ever having to hit the drop button. All you do is bring the claw behind the back row of plush and push them over (quickly so that time doesn't run out while you're doing this). This is SUCH a great technique because you're setting up the plush in the most optimal position to win. Like we talked about at the beginning of lesson 3, the best chance you will have at winning a prize is when you're going for a stuffed animal that is laying down.

The raking technique allows you to push plush over and gives you a shot at winning in one turn. It'll take some time to perfect this method but keep after it! In all my years of playing crane machines this technique has won me hundreds of prizes and is oddly satisfying.

Good luck out there!

How to Beat the Claw Machine: Tips and Tricks to help you Win Big!

LESSON 5

Conclusion

How to Beat the Claw Machine: Tips and Tricks to help you Win Big!

Claw School Diploma

Congratulations to the graduating class of (insert day and time here). You have put in the time, researched thoroughly, and learned what it takes to beat the claw. Thanks to the helpful guidance of professional claw player, Brian McKanna, you may now go out into the world and put all that knowledge into practice!

Now is your time!

One of the best places to play claw machines is at America's favorite super store, Walmart. They usually have two or three machines in both entrances. These machines are maintained by the same company nationwide, so there is consistency in their prizes and how often they are stocked. They offer a variety of pricing from a quarter to a dollar per play. If you start to master the plush claws, give the Treasure Chest claw a try. It's extra tough (and frustrating). Only a true master can win jewelry out of a claw machine.

Most Dave & Busters have easy claws, but the quality of their prizes is less than can be found in most machines. This is a great training ground for young claw novices and seasoned experts alike. It's always good

32

How to Beat the Claw Machine: Tips and Tricks to help you Win Big!

practice playing on an easy claw. Use that to your advantage each and every time you find one!

Next time you go to play the claw machine, I want you to pump yourself up. Go in with a winning attitude. Reassure yourself that you know what to do. **You got this!** Now that you're a full-blown claw machine expert get out there and put your new skills to the text.

Like a big daddy bird, I must let you go now. Fly, fly, fellow crane masters! It has been a pleasure sharing all my secret tips and tricks with you. I wish you the best of luck on your claw adventures and if you ever see me in the arcade, make me win you something!

33

How to Beat the Claw Machine: Tips and Tricks to help you Win Big!

How to Beat the Claw Machine: Tips and Tricks to help you Win Big!